WELCOME TO ARROYO'S

BY KRISTOFFER DIAZ

DRAMATISTS
PLAY SERVICE
INC.

NOTE ON BILLING

Anyone receiving permission to produce WELCOME TO ARROYO'S is required to give credit to the Author as sole and exclusive Author of the Play on the title page of all programs distributed in connection with performances of the Play and in all instances in which the title of the Play appears for purposes of advertising, publicizing or otherwise exploiting the Play and/or a production thereof. The name of the Author must appear on a separate line, in which no other name appears, immediately beneath the title and in size of type equal to 50% of the size of the largest, most prominent letter used for the title of the Play. No person, firm or entity may receive credit larger or more prominent than that accorded the Author. The following acknowledgments must appear on the title page in all programs distributed in connection with performances of the Play:

WELCOME TO ARROYO'S premiered at
American Theater Company in Chicago, IL,
P.J. Paparelli, Artistic Director.

WELCOME TO ARROYO'S has been developed as part of
the Hispanic Playwrights Project at South Coast Repertory Theatre,
Lark Play Development Center's Playwrights Week and Barebones at the Lark
in partnership with the Hip-Hop Theatre Festival.

SPECIAL NOTE ON SONGS/RECORDINGS

Dramatists Play Service neither holds the rights to nor grants permission to use any songs or recordings mentioned in the Play. Permission for performances of copyrighted songs, arrangements or recordings mentioned in this Play is not included in our license agreement. The permission of the copyright owner(s) must be obtained for any such use. For any songs and/or recordings mentioned in the Play, other songs, arrangements, or recordings may be substituted provided permission from the copyright owner(s) of such songs, arrangements or recordings is obtained; or songs, arrangements or recordings in the public domain may be substituted.

WELCOME TO ARROYO'S recieved its world premiere at the American Theater Company (P.J. Paparelli, Artistic Director) in Chicago, Illinois, on April 15, 2010. It was directed by Jamie Castañeda; the set design was by Keith Pitts and David Ferguson; the lighting design was by Charles Cooper; the sound design was by Rick Sims; the video projections were by Resean Thomas Davonte Johnson; and the stage manager was Dana M. Nestrick. The cast was as follows:

ALEJANDRO .... Joe Minoso
MOLLY .... Christine Nieves
TRIP GOLDSTEIN .... Jackson Doran
NELSON CARDENAL .... Gregory Qaiyum (GQ)
OFFICER DEREK .... Edgar Miguel Sanchez
LELLY .... Sadieh Rifal

WELCOME TO ARROYO'S recieved its West Coast premiere at the Old Globe in San Diego, California, on September 25, 2010. It was directed by Jamie Castañeda; the set design was by Takeshi Kata; the costume design was by Charlotte Devaux; the lighting design was by Matthew Richards; the sound design was by Paul Peterson; the music director was Shammy Dee; the video projections were by Aaron Rhyne; and the stage manager was Elizabeth Lohr. The cast was as follows:

ALEJANDRO .... Andres Munar
MOLLY .... Amirah Vann
TRIP GOLDSTEIN .... Wade Allain-Marcus
NELSON CARDENAL .... Gregory Qaiyum (GQ)
OFFICER DEREK .... Byron Bronson
LELLY .... Tala Ashe

CHARACTERS

ALEJANDRO ARROYO — male/24/Puerto Rican.
Owner of and bartender at Arroyo's Lounge.

AMALIA (MOLLY) ARROYO — female/18/Puerto Rican.
Graffiti artist. Angry graffiti artist.

TRIP GOLDSTEIN — male/24/Jewish.
DJ/rapper at Arroyo's.

NELSON CARDENAL — male/24/Filipino.
Trip's DJ/rap partner.

OFFICER DEREK — male/22/African-American.
Rookie New York City police officer. New to New York.

LELLY SANTIAGO — female/24/Puerto Rican.
Suburban college student.

PLACE

Arroyo's Lounge.

The Arroyo family apartment.

A back alley behind the police station.

The Lower East Side of New York City.

TIME

2004.

A NOTE ON THE DJ BOOTH

The DJ booth should be visible onstage for the majority of the play. Trip and Nelson will play music and make comments from there throughout.

A NOTE ON MUSIC

The text suggests certain songs for certain moments in the play. While it's not necessary to use the exact songs mentioned in the text, the inclusion of music — current, evocative, popular music — throughout the piece is very important. All music should be sourced from the stage, not the sound booth.

A NOTE ON SCENES

Scenes are generally divided according to plot points — not breaks in the action. Scenes marked "continuous" are just that, and unfold in the same location with no interruption. There should be no blackouts, even when switching locations, unless noted in the text.

WELCOME TO ARROYO'S

PRESHOW

Trip and Nelson are onstage as the audience enters. They are playing upbeat party hip-hop from their DJ booth — this is the music we'll hear in virtually all the bar scenes, unless otherwise specified.

Lelly is seated at the bar. She's got books and notebooks and papers everywhere. She's clearly researching something. Messily.

Trip and Nelson pay Lelly no attention. And vice versa.

1

Lelly turns, addresses the audience.

Music stops.

LELLY. Kool Herc. *(Projection: Kool Herc.)* Grandmaster Flash. *(Projection: Grandmaster Flash.)* Afrika Bambaataa. *(Projection: Afrika Bambaataa.)* These three men are generally acknowledged as the forefathers of what we now know as hip-hop music and culture. With any justice, this esteemed group will someday include a fourth name: Reina Rey.

It has been said, by at least one hip-hop historian — probably less than five — okay, probably less than three — but definitely at least one — that in hip-hop's earliest days, there was a Boricua — I'm sorry, you might not know what that means — there was a

Puerto Rican woman — who could rock a microphone in English and Spanish with only herself as her DJ and no one's ever heard of her and that's tragic but at the same time it's astoundingly awesome and I'm getting overexcited and ahead of myself and okay I'll stop.

In 1980, just as hip-hop became hip-hop, Reina Rey disappeared. And no one knows anything about her.

If anyone ever cracks the mystery of Reina Rey, she or he instantly becomes one of the foremost experts on the creation of hip-hop culture; and she or he becomes an integral component of Latino cultural history; and she or he, at that moment of discovery, validates her or his entire existence, especially if she or he is, say, a nerdy little Puerto Rican girl with a lot to prove. *(Pause.)* I think. I might. Have figured. It out. *(She gathers her books and exits.)*

2

Trip and Nelson, playing to the audience. The music is back.

TRIP. Ladies and Gentlemen, you have found your way to the hottest watering hole south of Houston Street. My name is Trip Trizzy, this is my partner Nelly Nel, and we'd like to welcome you … to Arroyo's.
NELSON. *(Rapping.) Welcome to Arroyo's where the players play/we serve them black white purple striped straight and gay / you could hear the girls say on Avenue A /*
TRIP. *Trip Trizzy gets busy like his name was e-Bay /*
NELSON. *And we play the narrators, chorus, and crew /*
TRIP. *Trip rocks the mic right …*
NELSON. *And yo, Nel does too /*
TRIP. *It's true, so I'll repeat, we rock the mic right /*
NELSON. *You're in the Lower East Side and not* In The Heights /
TRIP. *We're all going on a trip to the NYC /*
NELSON. *No Jet Blue, just all of you, /*
TRIP. *Nelly Nel, and well, me /*
NELSON. *We're gonna take you straight back to two thousand four / pre-Obama call your mama 'cause we giving her more /*

TRIP. *And mopping the floor and dusting the shelves / is our boy Alejan —*
NELSON. *But we're ahead of ourselves … (The music shifts to an old-school track: think Eric B. and Rakim.*)*
TRIP. *So just throw your hands in the air / and get dirty like Double Dare / and if you like hip-hop or never heard it before/let me hear you say oh yeah…*
NELSON. *(And audience.)* Oh yeah!
TRIP. Oh yeah!
NELSON. *(And audience.)* Oh yeah! *It's time to do it old school / 'cause yo, we're on a mission …*
TRIP. *Nel, drop out the beat / so they could hear / the exposition …*
NELSON. *Here's a little story that must be told / about a Puerto Rican brother / twenty-four years old / he's our boy Alejandro / and he owns this place …*
TRIP. *He loves this spot like he loves his own face …*
NELSON. *The superstar of the bar …*
TRIP. *The Sphinx of mixed drinks …*
NELSON. *Tending bar so fast, I wonder when he thinks / see, he lives upstairs / and he works down here …*
TRIP. *And I ain't seen him out this building in like half a year. (Music out.)* For real. That dude don't leave.
NELSON. *(Speaking, to audience.)* At the sound of the scratch, it's six P.M., June fifteenth, two thousand four … and Mr. Alejandro Arroyo will unlock that front door. *(Alejandro enters from the apartment, walks to the front door.)*
TRIP. And when he does, this lounge — his lounge — will officially be celebrating its one-month anniversary. *(An abrupt loud scratch on the turntables as Alejandro unlocks the front door.)*
NELSON. Happy anniversary, Al. *(Alejandro walks behind the bar … and waits.)*
ALEJANDRO. Today's gonna be the big day.
TRIP. Hells yeah, Al.
ALEJANDRO. Today's the day that Arroyo's becomes the most popular lounge in Manhattan. *(More waiting. No customers.)*
NELSON. *(To audience.)* Today's not the day.
TRIP. Just one month ago, this place was the hottest hot spot in the Lower East Side.

* See Special Note on Songs and Recordings on copyright page.

NELSON. Only it wasn't a lounge. It was a bodega. The dopest, most no-frills-est bodega in creation.

TRIP. Everybody in the neighborhood came through here, either to buy cigarettes or lotto tickets or those little mint breath things you put on your tongue and your eyes get all watery and —

NELSON. And Al's mom was sitting right where he's standing now. Just one month ago.

TRIP. Only she wasn't behind a bar. She was behind the front counter. And then, one month ago … she passed. Al didn't take it so good.

NELSON. That same night, the bodega came down. It wasn't pretty. It was a rough night.

TRIP. The next day, he started building this very bar. We were right there with him.

NELSON. It's a dope little spot, right? We know. We're proud. But the problem is … we can't seem to get ourselves any customers. Hell, this is more people in here tonight than we've had all month.

TRIP. But patrons or not, we're open every night. The whole night. Al tells us:

ALEJANDRO. *(To Trip.)* The sign says six to four, then we're open six to four.

NELSON. And then we tell Al:

TRIP. Ain't like we getting a rush at three forty-five. *(To audience.)* To which he says:

ALEJANDRO. People need to know they could count on us.

TRIP. And we tell him there's nobody here to count on us and people won't just come through only for drinks …

NELSON. *(To Alejandro.)* … and yo, Al, maybe if we gave people something to watch, some entertainment or something —

TRIP. But Al don't like gimmicks.

ALEJANDRO. A deli needs to be a deli. A bar needs to be a bar. We do what we're supposed to do the way we're supposed to do it. The customers will come.

NELSON. And even though he'd never admit it, the subtext of that statement is:

ALEJANDRO. It worked for my mother.

TRIP. And we can't argue with that.

NELSON. So we keep working. Exactly six to exactly four, every night. By two minutes after four, me and Trip are long gone.

TRIP. But Al ain't. He's just getting started on cleaning. Wasn't no one here to get the bar dirty, but he's cleaning.

NELSON. Cleaning ain't even the right word though. He's sweeping, mopping, down on his knees scrubbing scuff marks you can't even see off the bar rail.

TRIP. Gets this place cleaner than a Justin Bieber CD.

NELSON. You're embarrassing. And it's not like he exactly could get away from it by going home. *(Alejandro finishes cleaning and heads upstairs to the apartment.)* He lives right upstairs.

TRIP. So his whole life right now is up and down, from his cramped apartment to his underperforming bar and back.

NELSON. And that's all he does.

TRIP. Every day.

NELSON. That's it.

TRIP. We got nothing else to show you.

NELSON. Bet you wondering why you came to see this play.

TRIP. You fucked up. We got nothing. *(Molly, at the police station.)*

MOLLY. Ma! Yo, Ma!

NELSON. Oh yeah. He got a little sister.

3

MOLLY. I gotta talk to you about your son, Ma. *(Molly begins to spray paint.)* That kid ain't got no life anymore. Go to work, clean the family. Go to work, feed the family. That's all he does, Ma. I tell him though. I tell him that shit kills you, then you dead, and nobody outside your little circle even remembers you. That's what happened to you, Ma.

It's a disease. You had it. And your son Al got it now. You gave him that deli, you gave him the fucked-up genes. You gave him your fucked-up heart. But me? I got the little tiny good part of you. I got the clear-headed DNA. The unblocked arteries. I ain't getting infected. I'm an artist. *(Molly finishes painting and steps away from the wall to reveal that she has written the name MOLLY, big and bold.)*

I'm the only healthy one ever lived in this family. *(She exits toward the apartment.)*

4

Alejandro, making breakfast in the apartment.

Molly stomps in.

MOLLY. Don't tell me I'm late.

ALEJANDRO. Did I say anything about you being late? I'm working, Amalia.

MOLLY. My name is not Amalia. It's Molly. I'm not late.

ALEJANDRO. I've been sitting here staring at paperwork since we closed the lounge tonight. I don't even know what time it is.

MOLLY. Me neither. I don't have a watch. I'm an artist.

ALEJANDRO. Right. An artist. Well, I'm a businessman, artist, and I've got work to do.

MOLLY. You spend too much time on that shit.

ALEJANDRO. Oh, how should I be spending my time? Scribbling my name on a park bench?

MOLLY. When was the last time you even saw a park bench?

ALEJANDRO. When was the last time you were home before daylight?

MOLLY. When was the last time you had sex? *(Silence.)*

ALEJANDRO. That got nothing to do with nothing!

MOLLY. Generations of Arroyos are disgusted by your lack of mack.

ALEJANDRO. I got game.

MOLLY. Oh yeah — you're a rock star pouring cheap-ass vodka.

ALEJANDRO. I serve quality vodka. I serve quality everything. And anyway, yeah — bartenders are like one step down from rock stars in terms of game.

TRIP. *(From the booth — to the audience.)* And a DJ is like a cross between a rock star and a bartender, so you know how we do. *(To a specific audience member.)* Tell 'em how we do, baby.

MOLLY. All right, if you say you get ass, Al … nah, I still don't believe you.

ALEJANDRO. I ain't asking you to believe nothing. I'm just trying to get this work done —

MOLLY. You know, you might have better luck with the ladies in your bar if, you know, you actually had some ladies in your bar.
ALEJANDRO. Fine. You want to talk? Let's talk. You need to spend less time out there writing your name on some wall that no one is ever going to see …
MOLLY. I always put my name where people could see it.
ALEJANDRO. And it gets painted over the day you put it up.
MOLLY. No, it don't. Not always. And, and, and, and … fuck you.
ALEJANDRO. Oh, what's wrong? Now you don't want to talk? I got an idea. Why don't you head over to that sink and scrub a dish for once, maybe do something to help out around here —
MOLLY. You scrub. Bartenders are one step up from dishwashers.
(Molly exits.)

5

Trip and Nelson, in the booth.

Molly, working on the graffiti she started earlier—her name, big and bold.

NELSON. Even before her mom passed, Molly was showing signs of rebellion.
TRIP. No smoking, no drinking, she wouldn't touch drugs. Baby Molly's revolution sprayed out the tip of an aerosol can.
NELSON. At first, she was like any other graf artist — covered her face, chose a tag that couldn't be traced back to her, did everything she needed to do to make sure her secret identity stayed secret. Until one month ago.
TRIP. Until the same night Alejandro tore down the bodega, actually. That night, Molly went out, no bandana on her face … and she went ahead and wrote her name. Big and bold and unmistakable. It was almost like she wanted to get caught.

6

Continuous.

Molly writes her graffiti.

Officer Derek enters.

Molly does not see him.

OFFICER DEREK. Freeze! Police!
NELSON. And then she got caught. *(Molly drops the spray paint can and places her hands on the wall.)*
OFFICER DEREK. Stay right there, drop the can, hands on the wall.
MOLLY. You're like two steps behind, son. Should be up to frisking me already.
OFFICER DEREK. Are you carrying any weapons and/or narcotics on your person at the current moment?
MOLLY. You sound all young. And you don't want to frisk me? I'm offended. *(Molly grabs her bag and starts to get ready to leave.)*
OFFICER DEREK. Drop the bag! Hands on the wall!
MOLLY. How long you been standing there looking at my ass?
OFFICER DEREK. I just got here. I mean … I haven't been looking at your … hands on the wall!
MOLLY. Be easy, big guy. I'm just doing some decorating. No need to aneurysm yourself.
OFFICER DEREK. Turn around, turn around slow, ma'am —
MOLLY. Don't you fucking call me ma'am. You see my name. You call me by my name.
OFFICER DEREK. It is not my job to show that kind of respect to some disrespectful little girl —
MOLLY. I am not some disrespectful little girl. I am *this* disrespectful little girl. *(Molly points to her name. She still has not turned around.)* Now you try that again and you get it clear this time.
OFFICER DEREK. Fine. Turn around … Molly.

MOLLY. Say it loud like I wrote it, so the whole Lower East Side can hear you.
OFFICER DEREK. Young lady, I understand that you're frightened. You've probably never been in trouble with the law before. But don't worry. It's my job to get you back on the right track.
MOLLY. You gotta be fucking kidding me.
OFFICER DEREK. Now. I'm asking you nicely, one more time —
MOLLY. Did you see me write my name on this wall?
OFFICER DEREK. You're standing there, got a can, claiming like you did it …
MOLLY. But you didn't see it. Did you, Officer?
OFFICER DEREK. Not you actually doing it, but —
MOLLY. — Then I'm leaving, because you got … *(Molly spins, makes eye contact with Officer Derek for the first time. Love at first sight.)* Nothing. *(They freeze. The DJs play some kind of love song. Blackout on the police station.)*

7

Nelson, alone in the booth.

NELSON. The role of the grizzled but lovable senior officer will be played tonight by Mr. Trip Goldstein. *(Trip, at the bar, wearing a police hat. Alejandro, behind the bar.)*
TRIP. *(As The Officer. To Alejandro.)* She's got the rookie slipping over his own drool! I'm ready to hop on the CB and let all units know we got a riot about to unfold — a laugh riot! HA!
NELSON. *(To audience.)* That dude is mad grizzled, but surprisingly lovable.
TRIP. You walk back there — you know, that's where we go to smoke — and you got the whole picture in front of you. She's standing there, can of paint, guilty like Gilfrey, if you know what I mean … *(Molly, in the same spot we left her, staring into Officer Derek's eyes. He's standing there, hand on his gun, jaw scraping the ground like a loose muffler …)* Officer Derek, still staring at Molly. And the kicker — the be all kicker to end all kickers — is right over her shoulder, right

15

in his eyeline … there's her name on the wall. Molly's name, still on the wall.

ALEJANDRO. On the police station wall?

TRIP. On the back wall, yessiree. But eh, don't worry, in my mind, it's victimless crime. Worse things kids could be doing than writing graffiti. Even adds some color to the place, gives me something to read between puffs. And walking in on the two of them staring all google-faced? Better than *Dawson's Creek.*

ALEJANDRO. Wouldn't have pegged you for a *Dawson's Creek* fan.

NELSON. *(From the booth.)* He cried when it went off the air.

TRIP. *(As himself.)* Fuck you, man. I'm in character. *(As The Officer.)* So I walk into the parking lot … *(Trip, still as The Officer, walks over to the police station, where Molly and Officer Derek have not moved, have not taken their eyes off each other.)* Hey, rookie — we wanna sign you up for the squad softball team. Figure those fire department guys see your name on the roster and go running off with their hoses between their legs.

OFFICER DEREK. *(Turning away from Molly, embarrassed.)* I don't play baseball.

TRIP. We don't need you to play. We just need the name. *(Noticing Molly.)* Oh, I see you ran into our neighborhood redecoration specialist. It's all wrong, Molly. We asked for two coats, off-white. Let me get you the right paint, kid.

MOLLY. I don't know what you're talking about. I don't know anything about paint. I definitely don't know anything about this beautiful, stunning, perfect piece on this boring old wall. I don't know nothing about nothing.

TRIP. I guess somebody else wrote your name on this wall.

MOLLY. *(Fake sweet.)* That's not my name. My name is Amalia. I didn't do nothing. Ask your boy right there. *(To Officer Derek.)* Come on — you know I didn't do nothing. Tell him I didn't do nothing.

TRIP. You gotta show a little more respect, Amalia — didn't the rookie here tell you who he is? You're dealing with a celebrity …

OFFICER DEREK. I'm not a fucking celebrity. I'm a police officer. *(Silence.)* I saw some girl. I can't say if it was her. *(Pause.)* I guess we have to let her go, huh? *(Molly and Derek share a moment. Neither one of them speaks. Neither one would know what to say. Molly exits. Trip stares at Officer Derek, then breaks into laughter and returns to the booth. Officer Derek calls after the Senior Officer.)* I didn't see her do it. *(He redirects his conversation to Alejandro at the bar.)*

8

Continuous. Alejandro and Officer Derek, at the bar.

ALEJANDRO. If you didn't see it, you didn't see it.
OFFICER DEREK. If I didn't see it, I didn't see it.
ALEJANDRO. And what did you see?
OFFICER DEREK. I saw her. But not doing anything. I earned my uniform. I can handle New York. I can handle anything. And definitely some cute girl — I don't care how cute she is. And she's not. Cute. Not. Not cute. *(Alejandro slides a beer in front of Officer Derek.)*
ALEJANDRO. Guinness. Good for nerves.
OFFICER DEREK. Nerves? I don't have nerves. I have nerves, nerves-of-steel nerves, and, and, and she broke the law, and, and, and that's what I'm here to talk to you about. That.
ALEJANDRO. We got all night to talk about Molly. Drink up.
NELSON. *(Interrupting the action. To audience.)* Yo, chill, chill, chill for one second. Y'all don't even realize what you saw my boy do right there.
TRIP. Let me run the track back so we could give the ill alternate DVD commentary. *(Trip winds a record back and the scene resets to the beginning.)*
ALEJANDRO. You didn't see it, you didn't see it.
TRIP. *(Speaking over Officer Derek's lines.)* Right from jump, he puts himself on this guy's side. Two minutes ago, they never seen each other before. Now Al's his biggest ally.
ALEJANDRO. And what did you see?
NELSON. People who sit at the bar always want to talk about they self. Al always gives them that opportunity. First time you say a word to him, he's asking you for your story.
TRIP. And the thing is, look at his face. He's focused on what the cop is telling him. And it's not because he's talking about Al's sister. Al's attention would be on lock even if this guy was talking about President Taft getting stuck in the White House bathtub. True story. Google that motherfucker. *(Alejandro slides a beer in front of Officer Derek.)*

17

ALEJANDRO. Guinness. Good for nerves.

NELSON. Soon as that boy gets tense, Al's ready to chill him out. Slip him a beer, slow the kid down. Last thing you need in new bar like this is a agitated cop.

ALEJANDRO. We got all night to talk about Molly. Drink up.

NELSON. Yo, that's my favorite. Play it again, Trip.

ALEJANDRO. We got all night to talk about Molly. Drink up.

TRIP. Naw — I wanna play it even one more time.

ALEJANDRO. We got all night to talk about Molly.

TRIP. He ain't got no intention of talking about Molly. And the cop ain't looking for the end of a conversation anyway. You don't go to a bar to get your problem solved; you just want someone to listen to you. Al listens. That's what he does.

NELSON. And then this next move:

ALEJANDRO. Drink up.

NELSON. My man is only trying to make you drink faster so you buy more alcohol.

TRIP. And you don't even realize it.

NELSON. And you wouldn't mind if you did.

TRIP. 'Cause our boy is that damn good. So then two questions: how can he be so good down here with complete strangers … and such a mess upstairs with his baby sister?

NELSON. And more importantly: How can he so good down here with complete strangers … and we still don't hardly have customers?

TRIP. Now that question we can answer. In the next scene. (*Back to the regular scene.*)

OFFICER DEREK. I don't know how you can be so calm, and serve drinks, in the face, of this news, about your sister and her, and her, disregard, complete disregard for the law …

ALEJANDRO. Two peanuts walking down the street. One was a salted. (*Silence.*) Bar joke. And a cop joke too, I guess. (*Silence.*) You take things too seriously, buddy. What's your name?

OFFICER DEREK. People think graffiti is a small problem, but, but, but have you ever heard of the Broken Windows Theory? Quality of life crimes — like graffiti — destroy neighborhoods, destroy businesses —

ALEJANDRO. You know what keeps neighborhoods and business working, buddy? Personal relationships. That's why I make sure I get to know my customers. What their names are, what they drink, who they're dating —

OFFICER DEREK. — I'm not dating anyone.

ALEJANDRO. I'm not asking you out. I'm just looking for your name.

OFFICER DEREK. Okay. I'm Derek.

ALEJANDRO. You got a last name, Officer Derek? *(Pause.)*

OFFICER DEREK. This is a serious outreach that I'm making to you for your sister's sake, and I don't need to be belittled, or disrespected, or —

ALEJANDRO. No, no — who's gonna belittle you, yo? I got nothing but respect — and respect like I got for you deserves a full name. *(Silence.)* I could wait a long time. *(Silence.)* A real long respectful time.

OFFICER DEREK. Okay. Okay. My last name's … okay. My last name is … Jeter. *(Silence.)*

ALEJANDRO. Derek. Like Eric with a D?

OFFICER DEREK. Yes.

ALEJANDRO. And Jeter. Like Eater with a J?

OFFICER DEREK. Yes. *(Silence.)* Derek Jeter, NYPD. *(Silence.)* And your sister doesn't need to know that. And no, I'm not a Yankees fan. I'm from Boston. Outside Boston. Ashland — the suburbs. And I've heard all the jokes, so don't make them, because they're not original, and they're disrespectful to me, not only as a human being, but as a member of the finest law enforcement unit in the United States, who happens to be doing a pretty damn good job of protecting you and serving you even if no one wants to give me any credit for it. *(Silence.)*

ALEJANDRO. Okay. *(Pause.)* Derek Jeter, NYPD — don't forget why you are where you are. You're in the best bar in the Lower East Side. You're not here on business. You're definitely not here to talk about my family — *(The front door flies open. Lelly enters. It's a big theatrical moment. Maybe she's backlit. The entire attention of the audience should be drawn to her.)*

LELLY. *(To audience.)* Elisabeth Arroyo probably moved to the Lower East Side sometime in the early '80s — but you can't really confirm that, and that's kinda phenomenally awesome. You can confirm that she got a job in a deli, worked there for twenty years, and eventually became its owner, two months before she died, which was roughly One Month Before Today.

She was an institution down here. I used to buy Pop Rocks and baseball cards from her — okay, that's personal information, not academic. Forget I even mentioned it.

She never talked about herself, so no one outside her family knew anything about her outside of that deli counter, but I've discovered two bits of mind-blowing Elisabeth Arroyo – related info that I wanna share with you. Okay?

Okay. One: Knowing that I have to out of nowhere spring this all on her son kind of makes me ludicrously nervous, so I keep reminding myself that this is good news, and he's going to love me for bringing it to him, only it's not news, it's just a theory, and this isn't about love, it's about history — the act of historicization is not about being loved. *(Pause.)* I'm not sure if I'm using the word "historicization" correctly. *(Pause.)* Oh. And um, Two: Elisabeth Arroyo's middle name was Reina. *(Back to normal. Back to the bar. Lelly enters.)*

TRIP. Yo Nel. Is that who I think it is?

NELSON. Oh fuck … why's she here?

LELLY. Alejandro Arroyo?

ALEJANDRO. That's me. I own this place. What can I do for you? *(Pause.)*

LELLY. Some day you and I are going to Grand Marshal the Puerto Rican Day parade on the first ever float commemorating Reina Rey and we'll look back at today and laugh. *(Silence.)* Shit. I didn't mean to just come in and come out and say it like that. *(Silence.)* I have to go. *(Lelly exits.)*

TRIP. Oh, hell no.

9

Still in the bar, but later. Officer Derek has exited.

Trip and Nelson, talking to Alejandro, who is still staring off after Lelly.

TRIP. Her name is Lelly Santiago. In related news, she's a skank-ass white girl.
NELSON. She's Puerto Rican, but she's a white girl. Trust me.
TRIP. Bet she got a tattoo on her back over her ass and everything.
NELSON. Probably a dolphin.
TRIP. Yeah. Definitely a dolphin.
NELSON. But more important, Al — check this out. Me and Trip been working for you since this spot came open.
TRIP. Even before that. We helped you turn this spot into a lounge in the first place.
ALEJANDRO. What you mean, "skank-ass white girl?"
NELSON. We were here the night you tore the bodega down —
TRIP. — and we were here through the liquor licenses and the paperwork and the supplier contracts —
NELSON. — and we'll be here, bro, we'll be here. But we're saying —
ALEJANDRO. We're not changing anything. We do what we say, and the people will come.
NELSON. I'm not saying we should change anything, but me and Trip, see, we got this hip-hop group thing on the side.
TRIP. We rhyme in our spare time, yanahmean?
NELSON. We focused, man. We work that shit. We live that shit.
TRIP. Fuck, I wrote Ghostface in as my vote for president. *(To audience.)* I know you don't know who Ghostface is. *Pretty Toney Album*, 2004. You better Google that motherfucker, too.
ALEJANDRO. Wait, wait, wait — what you mean, "skank-ass white girl?"
NELSON. Skank like skunk, mean she stunk like shit was dank,

And when you sniff the stank, slink away from the junk, punk. *(An afterthought.)* Ass white girl.

TRIP. See? We live that shit! Hip-hop, you the love of my life!

NELSON. The reason why you ain't had such good business lately is because … well, it's because you ain't give The Tripnel Cartel —

TRIP. Hot name, right?

NELSON. You ain't give us the mic in the club yet.

ALEJANDRO. I'm saying, though …

NELSON. Come on, Al! We got the beats, we got the lyrics, we got the love …

TRIP. We got everything you need to bring the real Lower East Side crowd back into your bar.

ALEJANDRO. It's not a bar. It's a lounge.

NELSON. Lounges ain't what the LES is looking for.

TRIP. Real motherfuckers —

NELSON. — motherfuckers from around here —

TRIP. — want to hear other real motherfuckers —

NELSON. — preferably other real motherfuckers from around here —

TRIP. — making real motherfucking shit —

NELSON. — like a motherfucker. Me and Trip can guarantee we bring the local Boricua market back.

ALEJANDRO. I'm saying, though — I still don't see why you call-ing her a skank.

NELSON. How you still even have Lelly Santiago anywhere in your brain?

ALEJANDRO. What she talking about us going to the parade for? I don't even know her ass.

NELSON. You know what we are to Lelly Santiago? We a science project. We a ant farm. She's dubious, son.

TRIP. How she gonna troop on in here from upstate exploring the LES outback for specimens she could show off to her friends like she the Crocodile Hunter … *(To audience.)* may he rest in peace.

ALEJANDRO. How you know so much — wait, how you know anything about this girl?

TRIP and NELSON. *(In chorus.)* We the chorus!

ALEJANDRO. What?

TRIP. Nah, we know cause she used to live down here, on Norfolk Street 'til, like, fourth grade.

NELSON. And even then she was taking the train to the Upper

West Side to go to school with the other dark-skinned geniuses that were too smart and too precious to rot away in public school with us juvenile delinquents and future grown-ass delinquents. I don't know how you didn't know her.

TRIP. First chance her family got, they hauled ass out the LES. And she ain't never came back until she realized that the boy-band frat boys she went to school with got all impressed that she was from the "East Village." This ain't even the East Village! It's the Lower East Side! But she don't know the difference. She's the worst worst worst of everything that I'm talking about: a Puerto Rican girl who left this neighborhood when it sucked and only comes back to claim it when shit becomes convenient. Gives your people a bad name.

ALEJANDRO. Hold up, hold up. How I'm gonna take Puerto Rican advice from Trip fucking Goldstein?

TRIP. Don't disappoint me, Al. It's like Rakim said: It ain't where you're from, it's where you're at.

NELSON. And you right here, Al. We got mad love for that. Now put my Pinoy ass on.

TRIP. And put that skank out your head.

ALEJANDRO. She's in my bar. I need to make her happy.

NELSON. It ain't a bar. It's a lounge.

ALEJANDRO. That's right. And if she comes back, I'll treat her like anybody else. Nothing more, nothing less.

NELSON. But yo, she's a —

ALEJANDRO. Nothing more, nothing less.

10

Molly, alone in the apartment.

MOLLY. You saw that, right, Ma? Wherever you are, you saw the way that a real woman handles her problems, right? I ain't cleaning no walls 'cause some cops tell me. And the only reason I ain't out there again bombing that shit right now is … *(Long pause as she thinks about it.)* It ain't 'cause I'm scared. And it got nothing to do with that cop. *(Pause.)* I ain't gotta tell you shit. You wanna know so bad, you shoulda still been here.

11

Continuous.

Alejandro enters.

MOLLY. Just 'cause I'm here before you don't mean I didn't come home late.
ALEJANDRO. I met a girl tonight, Amalia.
MOLLY. *(Genuinely excited.)* You met a real girl?
ALEJANDRO. Yup.
MOLLY. *(Remembering.)* My name is not Amalia.
ALEJANDRO. Her name is Lelly.
MOLLY. The fuck kinda name is Lelly? Let me guess. Her last name is like … von Hofflinger or something. Lelly von Hofflinger. The Third. What is she, a freshman at NYU?
ALEJANDRO. How you know she was in college?
MOLLY. If she was in your bar, she wasn't no Lower East Side girl.
ALEJANDRO. How you know she was in the lounge?
MOLLY. Where the hell else she's gonna meet you?

ALEJANDRO. Her last name is Santiago. From Norfolk Street. There's something about this girl, Molly. I mean, it ain't even that she's fine — I mean, she is fine — but for some reason … for some reason, she was like … salt.
MOLLY. She's like salt.
ALEJANDRO. Like she threw salt and it hit my eye, and I blinked and I blinked and I blinked and it wouldn't go, it wouldn't flush itself out. And yeah, that shit hurt — you got salt in your eye, it hurts — but … I liked it. *(Pause.)* Aight, salt's not the best way to explain it. But I can't shake her and I'm kinda fine with that. I just keep blinking and blinking and thinking how good that salt could taste once it comes out my eye. *(Pause.)* Forget the salt.
MOLLY. Big pimping, Don Alejandro. Big salty pimping.
ALEJANDRO. Forget the salt! You still never did the dishes.
MOLLY. Servants do dishes. Artists contemplate why servants allow themselves to do dishes.
ALEJANDRO. You know what? I'm not doing these. They'll stay here until you decide to —
MOLLY. I ain't deciding shit. It's just the way things are. Artists and servants, big brother. You're a servant, Mom was a servant — *(Alejandro breaks away. Maybe he slams a dish or shoves the eggs back into the fridge. Silence.)*
ALEJANDRO. I met your boyfriend the cop today.
MOLLY. I don't have no boyfriend. *(Pause.)* How you know about him?
ALEJANDRO. Arroyo's is the central nervous system of the Lower East Side. Anything happens from Houston to Delanccy, I know about it.
MOLLY. What, did he come into your bar and introduce himself?
ALEJANDRO. Yeah. He did. We had a big night.
MOLLY. He got no reason to be there.
ALEJANDRO. Well, now he does. He's a valued customer. And yo, it's better for you that it's him and not the last three cops I had in my bar looking for you. He ain't interested in arresting you.
MOLLY. Why the fuck not?
ALEJANDRO. I think my man got a crush on your artistic ass.
MOLLY. He does?
ALEJANDRO. *(Offering her a plate of food.)* Careful with the eggs. They salty. *(Molly pushes past him and exits.)*

12

Trip and Nelson in the booth.

TRIP. *(To audience.)* At the sound of the scratch, Al will unlock the front door, and Arroyo's will officially be open for business.
NELSON. You might have noticed we do this every night. Al's like that prime meridian clock. Always opens in 3 … 2 … 1 … *(SCRATCH … then silence. No Alejandro. They wait. They check their watches. They wait some more.)* He's late.
TRIP. He ain't been late once since we opened. *(Silence.)*
NELSON. I'm scared. *(Alejandro runs in from the apartment.)*
ALEJANDRO. I'm not late, I'm not late. We didn't open yet. I'm not late. I was upstairs thinking, that was all.
NELSON. Uh oh. What you think he was thinking about, Trip?
TRIP. What you think I think he was thinking about?
ALEJANDRO. I wasn't thinking about no girl, if that's what you're trying to say …
TRIP. Then how you think you know we think we know what you thinking about then?
NELSON. Yo, I wouldn't even expect her back, son. She's out her place down here.
ALEJANDRO. Whatever. I ain't thinking 'bout her. *(He goes back to cleaning.)* How somebody you don't even know is gonna come into your place of business, be like, "You and me, the parade, laughing, whatever"? Then how she's gonna be like, "Uh" and walk out, and now you think she ain't coming back to explain herself? *(Pause.)* I ain't thinking 'bout her.

13

Lelly, alone. Outside the bar.

LELLY. My dad doesn't think I'm doing real research. He says all I do all day is look at old party fliers and transcripts of other people's interviews with folks who were there, and yeah, that's all I do, but hey — I found Reina Rey that way, and I didn't just find her story:

I found a picture. One picture.

She had just gotten arrested, her hands are cuffed behind her back, and she's wearing a sweatshirt with those iron-on felt letters spelling out her name — and okay, this is the awesome best thing ever part — she looks like someone I knew.

She looks, somehow, like the woman who sold me my candy when I was a kid. How could I not follow that up?

(She enters the bar.)

This is a bad idea.

(She exits the bar.)

Okay. I go back in, and I explain who I am — no — I apologize for being weird, for being weird last time and for being weird in general. *Then* I explain who I am. Then I go ahead and hit this virtual stranger with the earth shattering news about his late mother and the history of hip-hop and the future of the world as we know it.

Sounds like a plan.

14

Continuous.

Lelly opens the bar door—again, it's a big theatrical moment.

ALEJANDRO. You're back!
LELLY. Sometimes I start saying what I'm thinking and I say it too fast to not say it even if I don't know what I'm planning to say next …
ALEJANDRO. I knew you'd be back. I was waiting to talk with you …
NELSON. Yo Trip, you remember this song? *(Trip and Nelson, watching this, begin mixing in recorded snippets of their earlier conversation with Alejandro into the music. Alejandro, sampled.)* "I ain't thinking 'bout her."
ALEJANDRO. Now if I remember correctly, last time you was in here you didn't end up getting a drink at all.
TRIP. How that song went, Nel? *(Alejandro, sampled. Music being made from the samples now.)* "I'll treat her like anybody else/any/any/anybody else/I ain't thinking about her …"
TRIP. That was the jam.
ALEJANDRO. All's I'm saying is that ain't nobody coming back here two nights in a row and not drinking nothing.
NELSON. What about this one, Trip? *(Alejandro, sampled.)* "Nothing more, nothing/nothing more, nothing/nothing more nothing more nothing more nothing less/I ain't thinking about her …"
ALEJANDRO. I know you didn't come back because of the music. And the way we do things at Arroyo's is to make sure every customer walks out happier than they came in, and I ain't sure your happiness increased much yet — *(Lelly puts her hand over Alejandro's mouth.)*
LELLY. I think your mother wasn't exactly who you think she was. *(Silence.)* I think you don't know who your mother really was. *(Silence.)* You start talking and I forget where I am and it comes out. *(She exits. Silence.)*

ALEJANDRO. *(To Trip and Nelson.)* We're closed. *(Alejandro exits up to the apartment. Silence.)*
TRIP. Now I'm scared too.

15

Officer Derek, at the police station wall.

He has a paint roller.

Molly's name is still on the wall.

Officer Derek suddenly spins to face the wall, drawing the roller, like a gun, directly at the spray paint.

OFFICER DEREK. This job's harder than hitting a baseball. *(He does it again.)* Nineteen million dollars you made this year, Derek Jeter. For playing a game. I'm down here. On the streets. Keeping people safe. Keeping you safe. *(He does it again.)* What have you ever done for anyone, huh? You learned how to inside out a fastball into right field for a base hit, made one nice backhanded toss to the plate, and suddenly the world's in love with you. King of New York. Dated Mariah Carcy. Not that I'd want to date Mariah Carey. But still. What do you actually do, Derek Jeter? *(He does it again. Building his confidence each time.)* 'Cause I know what I do. I arrest people. I'd arrest you if I have to. Oh yeah, I would. Maybe then people would understand that you don't really do anything for any-one. Maybe then people would appreciate people like me. People who enforce the law. I can already see the headline on the back page of the paper: "Derek Jeter arrested by … Derek Jeter." *(Silence.)* You should be the one getting rid of her name. You're good at it."

29

16

Continuous.

Molly storms in. Officer Derek hides the roller.

MOLLY. I don't know what kind of sick ideas you got about you and me and some kind of relationship, but you need to put that shit out of your head right now.

OFFICER DEREK. Back to the scene of the crime, young lady?

MOLLY. I didn't commit no crime. And I ain't no fucking young lady. You see my name right there on that wall. You call me by my name …

OFFICER DEREK. And I'd appreciate you calling me by my name right there on that wall. Police. Police officer. *(Pause.)* That's not my name.

MOLLY. I don't give a fuck about your name.

OFFICER DEREK. Really? You're the first person in New York to say that —

MOLLY. — I don't give a fuck about your name, but you better give a fuck about mine. Now turn your ass around and look at who owns this police station you work in. You see right there where it says my name? *(Molly jabs her finger into Officer Derek's chest to push him to look. Officer Derek grabs her wrist and holds it there, finger flush against his chest. Trip and Nelson, in the booth. Molly and Officer Derek, frozen, still visible.)*

NELSON. When me and Trip and Al was tearing down the deli to build the bar, Molly used to throw broken bricks at us if we pissed her off.

TRIP. One time they were checking Molly's hair for lice at her school, and the nurse accidentally stabbed her head with the chopsticky thing. Molly punched her in the eye.

NELSON. She hates cops.

TRIP. Shit. She hates people she likes.

NELSON. She hits people she hates.

TRIP. But a cop? *(Officer Derek, still holding Molly's finger to his chest.)*

OFFICER DEREK. I am an officer of laws. This is a place of laws. You have respect, you will, for this and for me when you come here. *(Silence.)*
MOLLY. I'm not afraid of cops.
OFFICER DEREK. Fear I'm not asking for here. *(Tense silence.)*
MOLLY. That rhymed. *(Officer Derek lets go of her hand.)* It was cute, Officer.
OFFICER DEREK. I don't need smart-assed comments that are smart-assed.
MOLLY. I don't usually get down with cute, but that was, I don't know. Kinda funny. I didn't expect you to be funny. You ain't so bad when you're funny. *(Long silence.)* You didn't paint over my name yet.
OFFICER DEREK. I'm about to —
MOLLY. — took a long time for you to get started —
OFFICER DEREK. — they didn't tell me it was my job to clean it —
MOLLY. — you don't know what your job is? —
OFFICER DEREK. — my job is arresting criminals, not painting and cleaning —
MOLLY. — why you gotta paint and clean then?—
OFFICER DEREK. — it's just today. —
MOLLY. — get demoted? —
OFFICER DEREK. — it's just today. —
MOLLY. — did they say it was just today? —
OFFICER DEREK. — they said to clean it. I'm going to clean it. —
MOLLY. — See, that's the difference between you and me. Cops tell me to repaint the wall, I ain't repainting the wall. They tell you to do it, your ass has to do it. You're a servant. I'm an artist —
OFFICER DEREK. It reminds me of you. *(Silence.)* Your name. It reminds me of you. Maybe I won't clean it. *(Silence. Molly calmly crosses to Officer Derek … and punches him in the face.)*

17

Trip and Nelson, in the booth. They've been watching Molly and Officer Derek.

They play "Mama Said Knock You Out" by LL Cool J (or some other suitable face-punching commentary music). *

TRIP. What? We're comic relief.

18

Alejandro, cleaning the apartment.

Molly stomps in.

ALEJANDRO. *(Immediately as Molly enters.)* Lelly Santiago. She used to live on Norfolk Street.
MOLLY. Oh yeah? Cool. I punched that cop.
ALEJANDRO. I take time out of my busy work schedule for her, and she's gonna start talking about about about — I got books to balance and stock to rotate and she's in there not even trying to explain herself —
MOLLY. You probably didn't stop talking about your bar long enough to let her.
ALEJANDRO. Don't tell me I wasn't listening. I'm a bartender. It's my job to listen. *(Pause.)* You punched Derek Jeter?
MOLLY. I might go back there and bust him in his eye again on principle.
ALEJANDRO. No. That's one of my valued customers.

<hr>

* See Special Note on Songs and Recordings on copyright page.

MOLLY. And don't tell me I should apologize, 'cause I ain't sorry.
ALEJANDRO. I'm downstairs working — the only one of us who is working, by the way, and this is what you're going out and doing?
MOLLY. And I ain't sorry, and it ain't like he would listen if I said sorry. And I got no reason to apologize for nothing anyway.
ALEJANDRO. Don't apologize.
MOLLY. And I don't need no advice from you neither.
ALEJANDRO. Don't apologize. Don't go near there. Don't apologize.
MOLLY. If they're gonna arrest me, I can't change that. Not even with an apology, which I ain't giving anyway. Right? That wouldn't change nothing. *(No response.)* Right? *(Alejandro exits to his room.)* RIGHT? *(A loud knock on the front door of the apartment. Molly storms over, opens the door.)* The fuck do you want? *(No one there. A photograph is taped to the door. Molly takes the photo off the door.)* Ma? This is you, Ma? You should have shown me this before.

19

Lelly, at the bar. Big and theatrical again. She has a notepad.

*A song like Aaliyah's "Four Page Letter" plays as she writes page after page.**

LELLY. I go all dumb when I try to say it out loud. She's his mother. So what if I figured out she was Reina Rey? I mean, if I figured out she might have been Reina Rey. I can't stand there and spew words at him and not expect him to get offended. So I figured if I just showed him the picture, maybe I wouldn't have to explain. *(Lelly picks up the papers and walks towards the front door of the bar.)* But you can't just tape a picture to a door and expect that he'll understand. Of course I'll have to explain. So I wrote him this four-page letter. I would enclose it with a kiss … *(Lelly pulls out a hammer and nails the papers to the door.)* but romance has no role in reformation. *(She exits. Trip and Nelson, dumbfounded.)*

* See Special Note on Songs and Recordings on copyright page.

NELSON. Did she just…?
TRIP. With a nail…?
NELSON. In my man's door?
TRIP. I … I got no words.
NELSON. *(To audience.)* Just … just go to the police station.

20

Molly and Officer Derek, at the police station, staring at each other.

MOLLY. Okay. I realize that … in cases like this … you might look, or you might be looking for me to say … certain things that maybe got said in the kind of house you grew up in, but in my family, and in the way I grew up, we never said … like … we never said … like — the way I grew up, it didn't matter if I was, if I was right, if I was wrong, it didn't matter, 'cause we fight. We fight. And you could fight with like hands or you could fight with like words, and then you sleep, and then everybody knows that everybody's wrong and everybody's … fine with that. It's a cultural thing, and if you don't understand, then, then, then you a racist motherfucker.
OFFICER DEREK. You're apologizing.
MOLLY. No. I'm not.
OFFICER DEREK. I was maybe kind of asking for it. I don't know what you're sorry for.
MOLLY. I'm not. And you *were* asking for it. But you were being kinda nice. For a cop. So maybe … you shouldn't have gotten hit. So … you know.
OFFICER DEREK. Surprising to me that it would come from a girl like you.
MOLLY. The fuck you saying, a girl like me?
OFFICER DEREK. You don't seem like the apologizing type.
MOLLY. I'm eighteen. I don't need to apologize for nothing.
OFFICER DEREK. Look — this is unusual for a cop to be this open while we're on the job, but — you know what I was doing when I was eighteen?

MOLLY. You were probably a fucking hall monitor. The fuck do I care?

OFFICER DEREK. I was an artist, like you. Not exactly like you — a photographer. When I turned eighteen, the Ashland city paper offered to publish one of my photos — not front page or anything. Page seven. But still. I was a kid. It was a big deal to get into the paper at all. And I was excited. Until we talked about the photo credit. The publisher made the same joke I heard everyday for the last few years: "Derek Jeter? He sucks wicked hard!"

Yeah, I know, it's real funny, right? But that's my name. And I don't know — I didn't really want the photo credit after that. So they ran the photo uncredited. And I stopped taking pictures.

My mom, she has the photo on her refrigerator, probably still. And she put a sticker on it, a label, and it says "photo taken by my son, Derek Jeter." I didn't even want her to do that. But I don't know. I guess it's pretty cool. *(Silence.)*

MOLLY. My mom was cooler than your mom. *(Pause.)* People, some people, think that my mom didn't do nothing but sit behind a deli counter, but she ran that deli. By herself. And she raised two kids alone, and she did it in the most shit neighborhood south of the South Bronx.

OFFICER DEREK. You didn't come here to talk about your mother.

MOLLY. *(Cutting him off.)* And maybe, maybe that doesn't sound like shit to you, but I'm not gonna let you not give my mom the credit she deserves. And look … *(She pulls the picture out of her pocket and stuffs it into his hands.)* She was like me, I mean, I'm like her. She didn't back down from no cops, see?

OFFICER DEREK. This is your mother?

MOLLY. Fuck yeah, that's my mom.

OFFICER DEREK. She's getting arrested.

MOLLY. Fuck yeah, she is.

OFFICER DEREK. For what?

MOLLY. I got no fucking idea. Who cares? Look at her — the cops got her cuffed on the sidewalk, and, and, and she got the look, the I-don't-give-a-fuck look, 'cause whatever they got her for, it was bigger than what those cops could ever do.

OFFICER DEREK. Your mom —

MOLLY. It's the same way right now. I'm doing better things than

you could even imagine. I'm an artist. My mom — look at that picture and tell me my mom didn't have artist in her.
OFFICER DEREK. Your mom —
MOLLY. My mom was a fucking warrior. Whatever she's doing here, that proves it. My mom, my mom, my mom …
OFFICER DEREK. Your mom was HOT. *(Silence.)*
MOLLY. Stupid. *(She pulls the picture away from him.)*
OFFICER DEREK. I'm serious! Look … *(He moves next to her, pulling the photo back into his hands.)* See, her eyes are all big and midnight black, and same color as her hair, and hair that long? Sexy as sex.
MOLLY. Shut up, that's my mom!
OFFICER DEREK. Serious! Look — and her skin. You have the same skin. This picture, with these handcuffs and the sidewalk — that's not your mother. That's you. *(Silence.)*
MOLLY. Stupid.
OFFICER DEREK. No, look. Put your arms back behind your back … *(He bends her arms behind her, as if he was handcuffing her. She resists.)* Relax. Put them back there, and tilt your head like this … *(He pushes her head to the side.)* And let me look. *(He continues to hold her arms behind her with one hand, moves around in front of her, and holds the picture up next to her head. They are chest to chest. Silence.)*
MOLLY. I look like her? For real? *(Silence. They stare at each other. That same ironic rock love song we heard before is played. They continue to stare. Molly stomps on Officer Derek's foot, then punches him in the face.)*

21

Alejandro, in the bar, cleaning.

Trip and Nelson, in the booth, talking to each other but at Alejandro.

TRIP. So Nel, check out this purely hypothetical but wildly dubious situation: What would you do if someone defaced your valued property in the most stalkeresque, dubious way imaginable?

NELSON. Damn, Trip. That does indeed sound dubious. I'd probably cut the skank-ass white girl right off.
TRIP. Shh — we keeping it generic. He doesn't need to be thinking about her.
ALEJANDRO. What are y'all talking about?
NELSON. Nothing, man. Nothing. *(Alejandro takes a bag of garbage out through the front door, returns … and sees the letter.)* We was just saying that in the unlikely event someone had damaged our door or something … *(Alejandro opens the letter, reads it, and heads straight for Trip and Nelson.)*
ALEJANDRO. *(Reading.)* "The value of familial obligation, be it communal, spiritual, or filial —" *(Silence.)* The hell kinda wack lyrics is this? *(No response.)* Y'all didn't write this? *(No response. Alejandro keeps reading, exits towards the apartment.)*
TRIP. *(To audience.)* We think we should let him figure this out on his own.
NELSON. He figures out she wrote it, he figures out she's crazy.
TRIP. He figures out she's crazy, he figures out we was right all along.
NELSON. And once he knows we're right, he's gonna know we should rhyme.
TRIP. This whole Lelly speed bump turns out better for us than we thought. *(Alejandro bursts back through the door.)*
ALEJANDRO. *(Reading from the letter.)* "Obviously we know that subjectivity is truth — that's just basic Kier … Ker … K …"
NELSON. *(To audience.)* Basic Kierkegaard. It's basic Kierkegaard. *(Pause.)* That's right. We're omniscient, baby.
ALEJANDRO. For real, y'all wrote this?
TRIP. *(To audience.)* How could he not know who wrote this?
NELSON. *(To audience.)* How could anyone not know who wrote this?
ALEJANDRO. Y'all know who wrote this?
NELSON and TRIP. *(Nervous ad-lib.)* Nah, nah, no man.
NELSON. Whoever wrote this, the whole thing sounds kinda crazy.
TRIP. Whoever wrote this, I'm staying the hell away from them at all costs. You too, Nel?
NELSON. Yup. You too, Trip?
TRIP. Yup. You too, Al? *(Alejandro is reading the letter.)* Al? You gonna stay away from her — or him, I mean, whoever wrote it, I mean — you gonna stay away from her, or him, too, right?
ALEJANDRO. Whoever wrote this is real smart.

NELSON. Real smart. Book smart. College smart.
TRIP. And to go through all this … they must want something.
NELSON. That person definitely got an agenda.
TRIP. An agenda to fuck up your front door.
ALEJANDRO. I bet whoever did this could really help us out with the lounge. *(Pause.)*
TRIP. Damn.
ALEJANDRO. It couldn't hurt to talk to 'em, right?
NELSON. Damn. Yo, you know what I'm thinking, Al? I'm thinking you should just trash that letter.
TRIP. Word. You got other things to be thinking about. Like … well, like you already know me and Nel could rhyme, but you don't know that we could do magic. *(Trip grabs the letter and crumples it up.)* Abracadabra, son! *(Nelson blows on the letter, and Trip throws it over his head behind the bar.)* See? Magic.
NELSON. *(To audience.)* Desperate times, you know? *(Alejandro runs back behind the bar and drops down out of sight, looking for the letter. The front door of the bar opens. Lelly enters, searching for the letter.)*
LELLY. Fuck. He's already reading it. *(Alejandro slowly rises from behind the bar, reading the letter.)* Fuck. You're already reading it. *(Trip and Nelson, speaking to the audience from the booth.)*
NELSON. Okay, we recognize that y'all might be interested in the little thing they got going on there, but me and Trip can't take all that dubiousness in one sitting.
TRIP. We gotta snap that shit into little dubious morsels to diffuse the dubious essence.
NELSON. And so, as protest, we step in and kick the action back to Baby Molly.

22

MOLLY. You saw that, right, Ma? You saw what he pulled — "Oh you look like your mom oh she's hot oh let me touch you." I'm showing him pictures to defend you, not for him to get close and comfortable. And he says I look like you in that handcuff picture? Nuh-uh, no offense, no way. Not Molly. *(She slams the dishes into the sink and starts washing them.)* And and and and he don't take my paint off that wall, because he knows, somewhere he knows that it could cut him loose, and that's all he wants to see is someone cut him loose, same way the whole world wants to get cut loose. But Molly can't cut your wrists alone, Officer — you got to hold your hands out! Hold out your chains and Molly's truth shall set you free! *(Molly holds out her hands, full of soap and holding a dish. She just now realizes what she's been doing.)* Motherfucker!

23

Alejandro and Lelly, in the bar, same positions we left them in.

LELLY. Fuck. You're already reading it.
NELSON. Cutting her off from the booth. *(To audience.)* Yeah, see, we're still not ready to listen her speak, so what I'd like to do now is … *(Lelly walks over to the DJ booth.)*
LELLY. Hey!
NELSON. Um. Hey. What's up, Lelly?
LELLY. You can't stop me from talking to him.
TRIP. Oh. Okay. *(Pause.)* Wait, wait, wait — how'd you even know we were talking about you? We're in a whole different theatrical reality! How'd you do that? How'd she do that, Nel?
LELLY. Everything that you've said about me — about the white girl, about abandoning the Lower East Side, about me having no right to come back here — it's all true. Except for the tattoo. It's not a dolphin. It's tribal. But other than that, you're completely right.
NELSON. That's right, we're right.
LELLY. But I'm here to change it. All of it. I'm here for redemption. *(Silence.)*
TRIP. *(To audience.)* What we'd like to do right now is perform the Sugar Hill Gang's classic "Rapper's Delight" …
NELSON. … in its entirety…
TRIP. … *en Español.*
NELSON. *Digo a hip-hop / el hippy a la hippity hip hip-hop —* *(Lelly unplugs Nelson's microphone. Lights out on the DJ booth.)*

39

LELLY. Fuck. You're already reading it. I was kinda hoping I could come steal it back off the door before you found it. And now it's all worse than I made it the last two times, cause you probably think I'm some stuck-up neo-white faux-ethnic girl who can only express herself in some over-intellectualized heady masturbatory mumbo-jumbo letter and oh my god. You have me rambling again. This is a bad idea. I should go.
ALEJANDRO. No. You ain't leaving. I got questions. *(Reading.)* "The personified manifestation of the unheralded parallel between literal and spiritual service ..." *(Pause.)* I don't even know how to ask a question about this.
LELLY. You know what? You're right. You deserve an explanation. *(Lelly pulls a plate of sushi from her bag.)* This is sushi.
ALEJANDRO. My explanation is sushi?
LELLY. I have to go slow to stay focused when I'm explaining myself, especially to you, especially about this. *(Starting again.)* This is sushi. *(Pause.)* What do you think about sushi?
ALEJANDRO. I think it's nasty.
LELLY. No, but what do you think about sushi?
ALEJANDRO. I don't know — it's fish and it's not cooked and it's nasty.
LELLY. I think about sushi, I think about Japan. It's an archipel-ago — I mean, it's a bunch of islands, so they fish. Fine, that makes sense. Then I think about the fact that they don't cook it. Then I think about crab roe. And seaweed. And wasabi and ginger. And yes, I know, I'm just exoticizing the other, I've read Edward Said, I'm familiar with orientalism. But wasabi and ginger? Where did that genius come from? I think about how what they eat affects their body types, and their body types affect the amount of energy they have, and their energy affects the way they live, and the way they live affects what they produce, and that affects what we pro-duce, and that affects what I eat, whether I turn around and eat sushi or not.
ALEJANDRO. You think all that? From sushi?
LELLY. To start, yeah.
ALEJANDRO. Damn. When the hell do you eat?
LELLY. And you're probably wondering what this has to do with you, and it really doesn't have anything to do with you, except that … well, lately I've been thinking about you the same way I think about sushi. *(Silence.)*

ALEJANDRO. How much Trip and Nelson paid you to fuck with me?

LELLY. I couldn't imagine having to be paid to fuck with you. I mean, you're a bartender. Bartenders do important work. You help teachers burn off the stress of mandatory testing and escalating violence with a beer and some good company. Big business gets done over rounds of shots. Babies get made in your bar — I mean, not made, but planned — I mean, not planned, but the process gets started and you start it.

ALEJANDRO. Yo, I'm a get my sister and you tell her exactly that same thing you just said.

LELLY. I have a lot to say to her. And to you.

ALEJANDRO. She don't do nothing but write her name on the police station all day. And I do all that that you just said. And she got the nerve to say all I do is serve drinks?

LELLY. Those drinks — and by extension, this bar — and by extension, you — make up a central concentric circle of this neighborhood, which happens to be one of the central concentric circles of New York City, which, as everyone knows, is the center of the universe, which makes you one of the central concentric circles of the center of the universe in a way, and oh my god why am I saying concentric so much like an arrogant neophyte college student and oh my god, neophyte? — I'm doing it again. I'll shut up now.

ALEJANDRO. You can't shut up — all I know right now is you think I'm sushi in a center circle.

LELLY. The fact that you're sushi in a center circle — it's concentric circle, but your way sounds better — all it means is that … all it means is this: What did you think of the picture?

ALEJANDRO. What picture?

LELLY. The picture from your door. *(No response.)* You didn't see the picture? *(Silence.)* I really have to go.

ALEJANDRO. You can't go! Now I got more questions about everything you just said …

LELLY. But you didn't see the picture. And that means you don't have the picture and without the picture, there's no way I can explain to you who your mother used to be. *(Silence.)* I'll be back. I promise. Almost gone. Try the sushi. *(Lelly plugs the DJs' microphone back in and exits. Trip and Nelson, in the booth.)*

NELSON. *(Singing) Arriba el boogie al ritmo de la boogedy beat …* *(Playing a recording of a crowd cheering.) Gracias! Gracias mi gente!*

24

Molly, angrily scrubbing the floor.

Alejandro enters.

MOLLY. If you say one sound about me cleaning this house, I'm busting your ass.
ALEJANDRO. I need a dictionary and a fork.
MOLLY. It don't mean nothing if I do the dishes — I just did 'em. Ain't no reason why.
ALEJANDRO. Did you wash the forks?
MOLLY. I washed everything. *(He grabs a fork from a drawer, then exits back to the bar — hardly even looking at Molly. Molly follows him.)* You ain't even gonna ask what happened? I ain't gonna tell you, but you could still ask.
ALEJANDRO. Yo —
MOLLY. I ain't gonna tell you!
ALEJANDRO. — maybe I should use the chopsticks. *(Silence.)* I'm saying, they give you chopsticks, they don't give you forks. They gotta have a reason for that. And maybe you don't use the chopsticks, you don't get the same effect or something. Maybe it don't taste the same. Maybe I don't need the fork.
MOLLY. I punched your valued customer again. *(No response.)* I ain't saying that's why I'm cleaning. I'm just telling you 'cause I know you want to know. *(No response.)* And I'm a go down there now and I'm a bust that motherfucker in the face one more time, and no way I'm apologizing — he's the one out of line. You supposed to arrest somebody, arrest her — don't start touching on her and getting all close and comfortable and looking at her pictures of her mom and — *(No response.)* I'm saying, that ain't why I'm cleaning. I'm just telling you.
ALEJANDRO. *(Never looking up from his sushi.)* I actually might eat this. *(Molly stomps out through the front door. Alejandro, chopsticks in hand, just sits and stares at the sushi.)*

25

Officer Derek and Molly, at the police station, staring at each other.

MOLLY. I'm sorry. *(Silence.)*
OFFICER DEREK. I don't believe you.
MOLLY. You know how many black eyes I gave my brother since we were kids?
OFFICER DEREK. I don't believe you.
MOLLY. You know how many times I apologized to him? Zero. I ain't saying it again to you. Far as getting injured in the line of duty goes, you're a cop. You got off easy. *(Silence.)* I do not say to anyone what I said to you. You tell me right now that everything is cool and everything is understood …
OFFICER DEREK. Fine. Whatever.
MOLLY. You believe me?
OFFICER DEREK. Fine. Yeah.
MOLLY. And I'm cool? With you?
OFFICER DEREK. Fine. Sure.
MOLLY. I don't believe you. *(Officer Derek, frustrated, goes to leave again.)* I'm playing, I'm playing. Thank you.
OFFICER DEREK. I have to go back to work.
MOLLY. I brought another picture. I don't have anyone else to really show it to, and you kinda dug the last one, right?
OFFICER DEREK. It was okay.
MOLLY. My mom had you tripping on your tongue.
OFFICER DEREK. It was okay.
MOLLY. I promise I won't hit you again.
OFFICER DEREK. I'm not going to look at it. *(He looks at the photo.)* This is the same picture.
MOLLY. You wouldn't have looked at it if I told you. *(He goes to leave.)* Wait. Why do you think she got arrested?
OFFICER DEREK. How would I know?
MOLLY. I don't even know either. But whatever it was, it was right. She was right. Look at her face …

43

OFFICER DEREK. She looks like you.

MOLLY. Shut up! Stupid. Way she looks right there, she believes completely in whatever she did. You even know how that feels? To be that right? About anything? And then to have a picture of it? And then to show it to your kids? Do you even understand that?

OFFICER DEREK. No. *(Pause.)* Graffiti is a crime. Next time you're caught, the police will arrest you. Goodbye. *(He turns to leave.)*

MOLLY. I still talk to my mom. She's dead. *(Pause.)* Her heart stopped working. She pushed it too hard. That's what I tell her. *(Pause.)* She doesn't talk back. I'm not crazy. I talk to her, and I tell her when I do something wrong and I think I wouldn't have done the wrong thing if she was around still. *(Pause.)* But nah, she doesn't talk back. *(Silence.)*

OFFICER DEREK. Maybe she does, but you don't know that it's her.

MOLLY. I don't know where this picture came from. 'Cause it was taped to my door. And my brother wouldn't have done that. And who else is there? *(Silence.)* I think she sent it to me.

OFFICER DEREK. She probably did. My mom told me one time that when she dies, she's gonna call my name. She's gonna call my name, and she's gonna tell me that she loves me, and she's gonna make sure I keep being who she raised me to be. I guess that's why I don't change it. Even though I hate it. *(Silence.)*

MOLLY. You think it's my mom? Seriously?

OFFICER DEREK. Seriously. *(Silence.)*

MOLLY. And you believe I'm sorry now?

OFFICER DEREK. Yes.

MOLLY. 'Cause I am.

OFFICER DEREK. I know … *(She kisses him. Hard. Silence.)*

MOLLY. You're not going to take my name down, are you? *(Silence.)*

OFFICER DEREK. You're kidding, right?

MOLLY. Are you?

OFFICER DEREK. This, this story, your mother, this picture, this, this, this all is about graffiti?

MOLLY. No, I was asking for you.

OFFICER DEREK. This is all so I won't paint over your graffiti?

MOLLY. No, I want you to keep it up for you, it's yours, you like it, I want you to have it …

OFFICER DEREK. Sucker me in, all sweet and apologies, after nothing but anger and cheap shots? I am an officer of law.

MOLLY. No, I was asking for you. I want you to keep it up for you … *(That same ironic love song again.)*
OFFICER DEREK. I am a grown man — fuck a cop — I'm a grown man. You're a kid, a kid who thinks you can flirt and smile and try to kiss and try to intimidate a grown man like a kid …
MOLLY. No, I want you to keep it up for you, it's yours, you like it, I want you to have it …
OFFICER DEREK. I don't believe you. *(He begins to paint over the graffiti.)*
MOLLY. STOP! That's yours! *(He continues to paint over the graffiti.)*

26

Alejandro, still staring at the sushi.

TRIP. *(To the audience.)* The role of the scholarly yet thirsty patron will be played tonight by the lovely and talented Mr. Nelson Cardenal.
NELSON. *(At the bar, as a customer.)* Hello there, barkeep. I've inhabited New York City for many a year, and I've recently heard tale of your prowess as both mixologist and conversationalist. As I now find myself in need of refreshment, both liquid and spiritual, I've concluded that you are precisely the man to see. *(No response.)*
TRIP. Al. Yo, Al! AL!
ALEJANDRO. Huh? What happened?
TRIP. Get ya mind out ya food, son. You got a customer.
ALEJANDRO. *(To the customer.)* What you think about sushi?
NELSON. I beg your pardon?
ALEJANDRO. This is sushi. What do you think about it?
TRIP. *(To audience.)* And yo — that dubiousity goes on all night.
ALEJANDRO. Nah, but I'm saying … what do you really *think* about sushi?
NELSON. *(Back to himself.)* Stop with that shit! You don't even eat sushi.
TRIP. You got a whole plate of it sitting there all night. You ain't touched it.
ALEJANDRO. I'm thinking about it.

NELSON. What you got to think about? You bought it, you eat it.
ALEJANDRO. Didn't buy it. Ain't saying I'm gonna eat it. Saying I'm thinking about it. *(Pause.)* What do you think about it? *(Silence.)*
TRIP. Oh. No. She got to you.
NELSON. She got to you. We told you.
TRIP. We told you. She's trapping you.
NELSON. You E.T. to her, son. She gonna do the science on you.
ALEJANDRO. Ain't no science — maybe me and her could play doctor, but that's it …
NELSON. Don't try to turn this into her being on your dick.
TRIP. That girl don't get on nobody's dick without telling you to turn your head and cough.
NELSON. You're being examined and you don't even realize that the little hospital robe leaves your ass hanging out.
TRIP. We actually had customers tonight too. Damn.

27

Lelly, outside of the bar.

LELLY. I thought we lost the picture. *(She holds up a photo.)* Thank God for scanners.

28

Continuous.

Lelly enters the bar.

LELLY. I found the picture. Well, I printed out a copy of it. Reproduction, not original documentation. Stop talking, Lelly.
NELSON. Yo, she's like our best customer. But she never buys a drink.
ALEJANDRO. You're back! Okay, tell them, these two guys back here, exactly how important a bartender is to the universe. Tell them like you told me.
LELLY. Very important.
ALEJANDRO. Sushi in a center circle.
NELSON. Oh. I understand for serious now.
LELLY. Can I show you the picture please?
ALEJANDRO. But here's my question though: If a bartender is so important, then by extension — see, I said that like you, "by extension" — then a lounge is so important, too.
LELLY. By extension, yeah.
ALEJANDRO. Then how come we don't get the kinda customer numbers we should be getting?
TRIP. How you gonna ask this suburban girl? She don't know nothing about Lower East Side nightlife.
LELLY. Your genius DJ is right. I don't.
TRIP. Yo Nel, she said I'm a genius.
NELSON. She got jokes.
TRIP. Oh. That was a joke.
LELLY. Honestly, all I know these days is hip-hop history. That's why if you let me show you the picture …
NELSON. You know what has four thumbs and is hip-hop history? *(Gesturing to himself and Trip.)* This guy and this guy. The Tripnel Cartel. We're history that ain't even happened yet. We're the future of history. What you know about that?
LELLY. Nothing.

TRIP. That's right. 'Cause if you knew something about hip-hop history, you'd know how to answer my man's question. You'd tell him if he put us on in here some night, we'd pack this place tighter than my rhyme scheme.
LELLY. Sounds like that would work.
TRIP. Now she got jokes again.
LELLY. I think that's actually a really good idea, Alejandro. The beauty of a place like this is unity — making people feel like they belong to something they can't get anywhere else. Local artists — that seems like a great way to get started on building a community. *(Silence.)*
NELSON. Yo, this girl is mad smart.
ALEJANDRO. I told you she was. And I told you she got ways to help Arroyo's get up on its feet. So, Lelly, you got a cool way to describe this idea? Like some kinda Japanese food term that could sum it up?
LELLY. I mean, no. Basically it's a community center. For adults. With alcohol.
TRIP. Wow. She is good. *(To audience.)* You know what? We think we should just leave the two of them alone …
NELSON. You guys should probably stick around and watch though. *(To a particular woman.)* Don't miss me too much, baby. *(Trip and Nelson disappear into the background.)*
ALEJANDRO. *(Can't contain himself.)* I have eaten the sushi! *(Silence.)* Now you got me spitting words out like you.
LELLY. You tried it?
ALEJANDRO. Took me a while, but yeah.
LELLY. You don't understand — when I ate sushi for the first time, it changed my whole head. It's so different, a product of a completely unique worldview, a different approach to not just cooking but eating. Not just eating, but life.
ALEJANDRO. Uh. Yeah.
LELLY. Sorry. Did you like it?
ALEJANDRO. You know how you eat sushi and it makes you think all those things?
LELLY. Completely unique worldview.
ALEJANDRO. It made me think, too. About how I can't believe you Puerto Rican and you eat that nastiness.
LELLY. Well, I am. And I do. *(Silence.)*
ALEJANDRO. But … it *also* made me think about how I had never even tried it, but I was convinced I didn't like it. And then I tasted it … and I was kinda right. It was ass.

LELLY. Here I am, rambling about unique worldviews and international culinary paradigms … and the sushi is ass.
ALEJANDRO. But … it was ass in a different way than I expected.
LELLY. So it wasn't as bad as you thought?
ALEJANDRO. No. It was worse. But it was worse different than I thought.
LELLY. All you have to say is you didn't like it.
ALEJANDRO. It didn't taste like I thought … so it could have tasted good, you know? Makes you think when the stuff you thought you knew was wack ain't really wack — at least not wack like you expected it to be. And that's kinda a whole new view of the world too, right?
LELLY. That's exactly what it is. *(Silence.)*
ALEJANDRO. So … you wanna show me that picture?   LELLY. Have you ever heard of Reina Rey?
ALEJANDRO. *(Silence. Pause.)* You go first.
LELLY. Have you ever heard of Reina Rey?
ALEJANDRO. Only from you. And since you the one mentioning her, she must be a major figure in hip-hop history or some shit.
LELLY. She should be.
ALEJANDRO. See? I got you all figured out, Lelly Santiago.
LELLY. Reina Rey was one of the first real party DJs. *(Trip and Nelson, in the booth, dressed as 1979 South Bronx hip-hop pioneers.)* Think about what that means: It's 1979 in the South Bronx, and every party you go to boy after boy after boy is on the turntables and boy after boy after boy is on the microphone and it's always in English even when it's one of the few Puerto Rican boys, and it's macho and it's gang jackets and it's all one perspective, and then this girl shows up, this woman, and she shuts out the sexist shit talk, and she fights her way onto the tables, and she grabs the mic, and she spits in English *and* in Spanish, and everybody *loves* her. That changes everything — she was *there,* at the beginning, and now no one even knows she existed —
ALEJANDRO. And you're going to show me a picture of her.
LELLY. And she was your mother. *(Silence.)* That's my theory. *(She hands him the picture. He looks at it. He'll stare at it through the following. Silence. Molly, dressed in old school 1979 South Bronx style herself … including a sweatshirt that reads "Reina Rey.")* Elisabeth "Reina Rey" Arroyo. The Bronx, 1977, '78, '79, birth of hip-hop. Your mom was there. At least I think she was. And if she was there …

well, that changes the world, really. *(Alejandro keeps staring at the picture.)* You don't want to ask how it changes the world? *(A classic early hip-hop beat plays. Molly takes over the turntable and the microphone in the background, rocking the party back in the day.)* If you can place a Puerto Rican woman at the dawn of hip-hop's creation, not just as an observer, but as a vital participant, you change the perception of all women's entitlement to the form AND you reshape the face of ethno-racial relationships throughout the Afro-Latino diaspora! *(Molly stops the music.)* I'm doing it again and I know and I'll fix it. *(Molly restarts the music.)* Okay. We know that there were women involved back then. We know there were Puerto Ricans involved back then. We don't really know the specifics of a lot of their stories. But I think I know the beginning of your mom's story, and you definitely know the end, and if we put them together and tell it in its entirety … *(Molly is directly behind Alejandro. Inches away. She reaches out to touch him. Alejandro hands Lelly the picture.)*

ALEJANDRO. I don't know who this person is. *(Molly disappears. Alejandro goes back to cleaning.)*

LELLY. *(To audience.)* Um. That's not exactly the response I was expecting.

ALEJANDRO. Listen, I don't mean to get in the way of your essay, your school project, whatever, but you've taken up a lot of time, and I got a lot of work to do …

LELLY. Alejandro, no one in the neighborhood remembers your mother being around here before 1980. And Reina Rey disappears from the South Bronx in 1980. No one knows why. I think she got pregnant and started a new life. Here in the Lower East Side.

ALEJANDRO. You should probably go.

LELLY. Alejandro, I need you. I can't do this without you. I mean, not just because it's your mother, but I mean, I'm the suburban white girl here, right? What authority do I have to tell this story? I know this is a tough time and you're grieving, and I can't even imagine what you must feel like right now —

ALEJANDRO. — That's right. You can't. *(Silence.)*

LELLY. Please. Just look at this picture for just one second and there's no way you can tell me that it's not your mother — *(Alejandro rips the picture in half without looking at it.)* I liked this place better when it was a deli. *(She exits.)*

29

Continuous. Silence.

Lelly, to the audience.

LELLY. I thought it was her. I knew it was her. And now he says it's not.
  He would know, wouldn't he?
  Fuck. FUCK.
  So now what? *(Trip and Nelson scratch a record. The scratch is ornate and kind of obnoxious. When it's all said and done … Lights up on Molly, alone at the police station. Exact same way we left her.)*
TRIP. Hey, if a narrator won't help out a fellow narrator, who the hell will?

30

Continuous.

Lelly enters, stares at the graffiti.

Silence.

MOLLY. I will. Fucking kill you. If you don't stop looking at that. *(Lelly keeps looking. Molly does not kill her.)*
LELLY. Can I just say that I love this? Like I crazy love this. I wish I had a camera. *(Pause.)*
MOLLY. Should have seen it before he … before the cops fucked it up.
LELLY. That right there is not fucked up. That right there is kinda brilliant.

51

MOLLY. It got a fucking hole in the middle.
LELLY. So do you! *(Molly glares.)* Please don't kill me. I mean, it's like … like there's a hole in your middle — not you like *you,* like you like everybody. I mean, I know I'm missing something someplace inside me — I think everybody is. And that's there. In what you painted.
MOLLY. You think I wanted there to be a hole in the middle?
LELLY. Doesn't matter. Like, look: The crazy thing about graffiti, it's considered one of the four elements of hip-hop, you know, one of the art forms that started the whole culture, and … the original graffiti writers didn't have anything to do with the music. They didn't want to be a part of some "urban" "culture" "movement" whatever. They just did what they did, and they ended up fitting in anyway. Without trying. They didn't even want to be a part of hip-hop, and now they're an element. So who cares what they set out to do? Look at what they did. *(Silence.)*
MOLLY. You talk too much.
LELLY. I know. I think too much. I'm a freak. *(Silence.)* I'm Lelly.
MOLLY. The fuck kinda name is Lelly?
LELLY. My brother couldn't pronounce Elisabeth.
MOLLY. That's my mother's name.
LELLY. Elisabeth Reina Arroyo. *(Silence.)* I'm not like a stalker or anything, so don't worry. I'm doing research — I was doing research. Tons and tons and tons of research. But. My thesis was wrong. I was wrong. Fuck. I was wrong. *(Silence.)*
MOLLY. How do you know?
LELLY. Your brother told me. *(Silence. Molly busts out laughing.)*
MOLLY. You did all that research, and you think you're wrong because my brother told you you were? Unless you're researching the best way to sweep up a bar, my brother can't tell you nothing. You're the one that did all that research, right? Maybe you're the one that's gonna accidentally become an element. *(Silence.)*
LELLY. I really wish I had a camera. *(Silence.)*
MOLLY. You wanna see a picture?
LELLY. You take pictures of your work?
MOLLY. I don't know who took it. It's a picture of my mom. *(Molly pulls out the picture. Lelly does not see it.)* She got writing on her sweatshirt. I don't know what it says.
LELLY. I do.

No lights in the bar.

TRIP.   Ladies and gentlemen, you have found your way to the hottest watering hole south of Houston Street. *(The bar lights start to strobe on and off — Nelson is standing by the light switch, flipping it up and down.)* My name is Trip Trizzy, this is my partner Nelly Nel, and … yo. The hell are you doing with the lights?
NELSON.   That's the strobe! We big time — we deserve lighting effects. *(Alejandro enters. Cleaning. Everything.)*
ALEJANDRO.   If I gotta change these earlier than scheduled, it's coming out of both of your paychecks.
NELSON.   Shit, like you can afford to pay us anything right now anyway.
TRIP.   But that's about to change, Al. The word is out about the big event. The whole LES is already excited about it.
ALEJANDRO.   Excited about what?
TRIP.   You know. This local artists thing. Or more specifically, this Trip and Nelson thing.
NELSON.   We been telling some folks some things, and they can't wait to come through.
TRIP.   It's what the community's been waiting for. Lelly was right.
ALEJANDRO.   She was not right. About anything. *(Silence.)* We're not doing it.
NELSON.   But Al …
ALEJANDRO.   A bodega needs to be a bodega. A bar needs to be a bar. We do what we're supposed to do the way we're supposed to do it. The customers will come.
TRIP.   *(To audience.)* And again, whenever he starts talking like this, the subtext is:
ALEJANDRO.   It worked for my mother.
TRIP.   And there's just no way to argue with that.
NELSON.   Unless … you get some kinda divine intervention. *(Alejandro has never stopped cleaning for a second.)*

Continuous.

The front door of the bar flies open.

Molly enters. Maybe it's backlit — maybe it looks exactly like one of Lelly's earlier entrances.

She's got spray paint. Lots of it.

MOLLY. I'm gonna paint your bar.
NELSON. *(To audience.)* Thank God for Molly.
ALEJANDRO. *(Stops cleaning.)* What?
MOLLY. — Your lounge. It's a lounge. I'm gonna paint it. I even already got the paint. Don't ask me how I got it, but I got it.
NELSON. Why you think we can't ask her where she got it, Trip?
MOLLY. Normally, a wise comment like that would get your ass kicked. But I feel good, and no, to answer your question, I didn't do nothing wrong. I didn't steal nothing.
TRIP. You just decided to buy bags and bags of paint and show up and try to throw your name up all over the bar — lounge, lounge, I know, lounge.
MOLLY. I ain't trying to do nothing but talk to my brother. But no, I ain't gonna write my name on any of these walls, even if the all of you got down and begged me. I got a whole plan for in here already, Alex, but whatever you wanna do, I could work with you. And I don't want nothing from you. I'm just a humble local artist contributing to the creation of my neighborhood's newest community center. For adults. With alcohol. *(Silence. Alejandro starts polishing the bar, hard and intense and angry.)*
NELSON. Okay. I think this is a family situation …
TRIP. Yeah. Me and Nel are gonna step over here and we just gonna … *(They exit quickly.)*
ALEJANDRO. She got to you.
MOLLY. Lelly bought me all this paint and we came up with a

whole plan to pay tribute to Reina Rey on every wall in this space —
ALEJANDRO. *(Still polishing the same spot on the bar.)* Why? Why would I let you do that? "Reina Rey" has nothing to do with us —
MOLLY. She was a woman and a Puerto Rican and an artist! How you gonna say she had nothing to do with me?
ALEJANDRO. She doesn't she doesn't … she doesn't have anything to do with the lounge —
MOLLY. She helped create hip-hop! That's all you play in here! *(Stopping him from polishing.)* And the fucking bar is clean!
ALEJANDRO. She's not … she isn't … Lelly doesn't have any proof that she's …
MOLLY. No, Alejandro, Lelly doesn't have any proof that Reina Rey was our mom. Who fucking cares? Maybe Reina Rey never had anything to do with us — maybe she got hit by a train in 1980 and that's why no one knows where she went. But Alex — no one knows where she went. And she might have come here. And she might have been our mom. And if not, so fucking what? Whoever she is, I loved hearing her story, and I want to celebrate it —
ALEJANDRO. No, no, no, you're not doing that, not in here, no, you're not doing that —
MOLLY. Why are you so fucking upset about this?
ALEJANDRO. Because our mother just died! *(Beat.)* Our mother just fucking died. *(Silence.)*
MOLLY. I know. *(Silence.)* If you really don't want me to paint in here, I won't. *(No response.)* Maybe I'll go make breakfast. *(She kisses him on the cheek, then exits up to the apartment. Alejandro goes back to cleaning for a second … then exits. Out the front door.)*
NELSON. Uh … not to make too big a deal out of this, but I can't remember the last time Al mentioned his mom.
TRIP. Or even walked out that front door. Promising, right?

33

Officer Derek, alone at the police station.

He is painting the wall.

This goes on in silence for a while.

Alejandro enters. He stares long and hard at the wall.

ALEJANDRO. It's gone.
OFFICER DEREK. Of course it's gone, Mr. Arroyo. Can't leave that kind of vandalism up on police property.
ALEJANDRO. Of course, of course. Just doing your job, right? But can I ask you something? Was it good? *(Silence.)*
OFFICER DEREK. I don't know what you're talking about.
ALEJANDRO. You know, I haven't seen any of my sister's graffiti since we were kids. She doesn't even know I saw that. She used to write her tag on the wall in front of our apartment building. She wasn't writing her name back then. Couldn't even make out what it said. But she worked hard on it, even back then. Me and my ma, we used to sit in the window and watch her sometimes. And I, I was like you, it's a crime, you know? I wanted to go out there and snatch that can out her hand. That was my ma's building she was writing on. That was extra work she was giving her. My mom already worked too hard. My mom worked way too hard. *(Silence.)*
OFFICER DEREK. Mr. Arroyo, I've got to get back to work —
ALEJANDRO. You know, but the thing was, my mom didn't let me go out and stop her. Said she had to practice somewhere if she was gonna be any good. Might as well be at home.
OFFICER DEREK. You mother must have known there was no way to stop her from doing it. You could tell. You could just tell. You could just look at her graffiti and tell that it was something she needed to get out into the world, and there wasn't any way to stop her from doing it, and when you saw that, the only thing you could do was to try to make sure she did it someplace where she'd be safe

and where people who saw it would respect it and value it and maybe even love it, even if they eventually had to clean it off the wall. *(Silence.)* That must be what your mother thought.
ALEJANDRO. Exactly. Must have been. So listen, yeah — I know you gotta get back to work. I appreciate you taking the time to listen —
OFFICER DEREK. Hey, I'm not a bartender, but listening's still part of the job.
ALEJANDRO. A'ight, well, you're still a valued customer, so come by whenever —
OFFICER DEREK. Mr. Arroyo — *(Officer Derek pulls a picture from his pocket and hands it to Alejandro.)*
ALEJANDRO. Whoa.
OFFICER DEREK. I know. She's pretty good, right? Can you, um, give that to your sister for me?
ALEJANDRO. I don't think so. You should give her this yourself. Next week. She's gonna have some art up in my lounge. I don't think I dig blank walls so much no more. *(Alejandro exits.)*

34

Lelly, holding a manila envelope.

LELLY. So. It's about a week after the last time I was in Arroyo's, and I haven't been back yet, because, well, you saw how things ended last time. But I'm heading back tonight, and there are two reasons why. One: Tonight is Arroyo's first ever Local Artists Night, featuring the smooth sonic stylings of … The Tripnel Cartel!
TRIP and NELSON. *(Ad-lib from offstage.)* Aww yeah, you know it!
LELLY. — and, more importantly, visual art compliments of one Ms. Amalia Arroyo. So that's one reason. And the second reason is that I just received this envelope, which I have yet to open, and which contains hard and fast proof of the true identity of Reina Rey. So I kind of have to go back now, don't I? *(She heads towards the bar, then stops.)* Oh … and thanks for being such great listeners.

35

Lelly enters the bar.

It's covered in Molly's paintings.

There's a party going on.

Alejandro is at the bar.

LELLY. Wow. These are amazing. Molly did all this?
ALEJANDRO.   All about your girl Reina Rey. Just like you planned right? Whether she's got anything to do with this place or this family or not, she's up in here now. There you go, college girl. We're helping you change the world.
LELLY. I knew this was a bad idea.
ALEJANDRO. And now you wanna freak out and leave.
LELLY. I do. But I can't.
ALEJANDRO. Listen — as you can see, we got a busy night in here tonight, so excuse me —
LELLY. I found out who she was.

I found out who the woman who got arrested was. I put in a request for some police records, and they sent to me. I haven't looked yet, but the answer is right in here. And hold on, don't say anything yet because you know how I get.

Thanks.

I could take the information in this envelope and publish it, and then I'd be the prodigal daughter, coming back to the Lower East Side as a conquering hero —it would be like I had never left. Scholars and historians and experts from all over the country — maybe all over the world — would come to me, goofy little Elisabeth Santiago, the foremost authority on this one particular aspect of Puerto Rican culture. And they would never, for a second, question if I was Puerto Rican enough to claim ownership.

But I'm not going to open it. You are. *(Lelly hands him the envelope.)*

58

ALEJANDRO. Me? Why me?

LELLY. There is a strong possibility that this envelope contains pretty important information about your mother. And when I first came here to talk to you about it, I knew that she had just passed, and I barged in here anyway, thinking that I was about to change the world and that it was all so important that it couldn't even wait long enough for me to ask you how you were handling your loss. And it's not nearly that important.

So. When you're ready, you can open this envelope, and we can discuss what's inside. Until then … Hi. My name is Lelly. I'm sorry to hear about your mother's passing. And if you'd like to talk about it, I'm more than ready to listen. *(A beat. Or two. Molly enters, all dressed up, and grabs a microphone.)*

MOLLY. Excuse me, excuse me: even you two, yo, if I could have you attention: I just wanted to thank you all for coming out tonight, for filling up Arroyo's and supporting local artists like me. Thank you all for checking out the murals on the wall — I'm glad I could share my work with so many people. And now I got the honor to introduce the reason a lot of you came through tonight: for the first time at Arroyo's … ladies and gentlemen, the Tripnel Cartel!

TRIP and NELSON. *(Ad-lib.)* Yeah, yeah, yeah, you knew it was just a matter of time … Lower East Side, let me know if you're ready! Yeah, I think they're ready …

TRIP. *(Rapping.)* *So just throw your guns to the front/Pull out your weed and roll a blunt …*

NELSON. *If you're ready for hell / with Tripnel Cartel / let me hear you yell …* (Officer Derek slams the front door shut loudly and thrusts his badge in the air.)

OFFICER DEREK. Freeze! Police! *(Music out.)*

TRIP. We ain't got no weed! We studio gangstas! It's just a image! *(Silence.)*

OFFICER DEREK. A joke. That's what that was. A joke. *(To Trip and Nelson.)* You can play the music again. Please. *(Trip and Nelson turn the music back on. Officer Derek turns to Molly.)* I did that only because I didn't know what to say. A joke. It was. I saw you had a drink, and that is illegal and all. I'm not going to say anything about it, though. I didn't really expect you to laugh. I brought you something. *(He pulls out a picture, holds it towards her. No response.)* It's a picture. I don't have pictures of my mom or my family like you do. I don't have that many pictures at all, really. I thought you might like this one. It's a picture of your name. *(No response.)*

I took it before ... before we, uh, cleaned the wall. A whole roll I took. This one came out really well, though. And the cool thing, for me at least, is if you flip it over, I put a little photo credit on it. "Photo by Officer Derek Jeter." *(He tries to hand her the picture, but she doesn't take it.)* I won't make you take it. *(He turns to leave.)* What you did in here, on the walls, it's beautiful, don't get me wrong — but you really shouldn't stop writing your name. *(He's almost gone.)*
MOLLY. Hold up. *(Molly calmly crosses to Officer Derek.)*
TRIP. *(From the booth, to the bar crowd.)* Yo, we don't just play hip-hop in here — we got that new techno remix too! *(That same ironic love song plays one more time. Molly stares at Officer Derek.)*
MOLLY. Let me get that picture. *(He hands it to her. She keeps staring at him. She never looks at the picture.)* Thanks. *(Silence as they continue to stare at each other. Maybe they even break a smile.)*
OFFICER DEREK. Well, that's all I came here to do, so —
MOLLY. You could stay, if you want —
OFFICER DEREK. Thanks. But I'm on duty. *(Officer Derek tips his hat, smiles, exits. Molly walks straight over to Alejandro and Lelly.*
MOLLY. I'm going upstairs. It's not because of him. And you better not follow me. *(Molly exits. She leaves the picture on the bar.)*
ALEJANDRO. I know we're talking but —
LELLY. Yeah ... you should probably follow her.
ALEJANDRO. You're not going to leave again, are you?
LELLY. Not a chance. I'm going to sit right here and enjoy the center circle. *(A beat. Alejandro exits up into the apartment after Molly. A beat. Lelly takes it all in. She looks at the photo. She was right. It's better without the hole. Lelly sits and enjoys the whole scene.)*

36

Trip and Nelson, in the booth, to the audience.

NELSON. The week after that first Local Artists Night, Arroyo's held its second Local Artists Night.
TRIP. The week after that, we did it again.
NELSON. And slowly —
TRIP. — but surely —
NELSON. — and just like we said would happen if Al let us rhyme —
TRIP. — folks started coming to Arroyo's from miles around. And even now, six years later, if you find yourself in Manhattan —
NELSON. — and you make your way down to Eldridge Street, you'll find Alejandro behind the bar — *(Alejandro, behind the bar.)*
TRIP. And me and Nel on the ones and twos.
NELSON. And depending on the night, you might just find another familiar face or two enjoying the Lower East Side's oldest community center —
TRIP. — for adults —
TRIP and NELSON. — with alcohol. *(Somewhere in the previous three lines: Molly, Lelly, and Derek, all in the bar. It's low-key. But it's happy.)*
TRIP. So that's it. That's all we got. *(They turn up the music and ignore the audience, as if the show was over.)*
NELSON. No, for real this time. You better get out there and beat the crowd. You know how parking can get out here after a show. *(They go back to the music.)*
TRIP. Nah, we just fucking with you. You still wanna know what's in that envelope, right?
NELSON. Reina Rey in all her glory. Was she Al and Molly's mom? She somebody else that just up and vanished? *(The envelope is still on the bar.)* You think it matters?
TRIP. Or maybe it just matters if she's really a major figure in the birth of this artform, this culture, this hip-hop that I love … or if

maybe Lelly didn't even know what she was talking about. Maybe she made the whole thing up.

NELSON. Wow — that's a brilliant theory I hadn't even considered, Mr. Goldstein.

TRIP. You better consider it, Mr. Cardenal.

NELSON. Consideration is in effect. And the answer — that's right here in this envelope. *(Long pause. Then to the audience.)* But you could do your own research. I'm a DJ. I'm here to party. *(They turn the volume on that upbeat party hip-hop way up.)*

End of Play

PROPERTY LIST

Books, notebooks, papers
Spray paint, graffiti bag
Police hat
Breakfast food, utensils
Beers
Plate of food, eggs
Cleaning rags, spray cleaner
Paint roller
Photo and copies
Notepad, papers
Hammer and nail
Bag of garbage
Dishes, dishrag, soap
Bag, sushi
Fork, chopsticks
Manila envelope
Photo of "Molly" graffito